METHODOLOGY OF EVANGELISM

SESSION 5

INTERFACING EVANGELISM and DISCIPLESHIP

DR. AARON R. JONES
Foreword by Dr. Timothy M. Hill

Interfacing Evangelism and Discipleship

WORKBOOK

Methodology of Evangelism

Dr. Aaron R. Jones

Interfacing Evangelism and Discipleship - Methodology of Evangelism

Copyright © 2018 by Dr. Aaron R. Jones

Printed in the United States of America

Published by Kingdom Publishing, LLC, Odenton, MD 21113

All rights reserved. No part of this book may be reproduced or transmitted in any form or by any means, electronic or mechanical, including photocopying, recording or by any information storage and retrieval system without written permission from the author, except for the inclusion of brief quotations in a review.

All scripture quotations are from the King James Version of the Bible. Thomas Nelson Publishers, Nashville: Thomas Nelson, Inc. 1972

Editor: Sharon D. Jones

Graphic Designer: Janell McIlwain – JM Virtual Concepts

                Tiara Smith

ISBN 978-1-947741-20-1

Table of Contents

Interfacing Evangelism and Discipleship **Sessions** 1

Foreword 2

C.A.P.S. Paradigm 3

The Great Commission 5

Component #1 **Care** 7

Component #2 **Aware** 11

Component #3 **Prepare** 16

Component #4 **Share** 21

Two By Two Rule 25

Types of Evangelism 28

About the Author

Contact Page

Interfacing Evangelism and Discipleship
Sessions

Session 1—**Introduction and Philosophy**

Session 2—**5 Principles to Encourage Evangelism**

Session 3—**Components of Evangelism**

Session 4—**Bait for Evangelism**

Session 5—**Methodology of Evangelism**

Session 6—**Church Planting Produces Evangelism and Discipleship**

Session 7—**Babes in Christ**

Session 8—**Components of Discipleship**

Session 9—**Evangelism and Discipleship Plan**

Session 10—**Spirit of Forgiveness**

Foreword

When God calls a man of faith and fortitude to a specific purpose in the building of His Kingdom, He uses an individual like Dr. Aaron Jones.

Feeling the urgency of the hour, Dr. Jones has shaped his participation in the FINISH Commitment by emphasizing the merging of evangelism and discipleship strategies to assist churches and individuals in their quests to effectively reach the lost. As Senior Pastor of New Hope Church of God, he is well-aware of what it takes to affect the Great Commission of our Lord.

Dr. Jones' desire is to instruct others on how to deliberately make an impact on winning souls and then discipling them for powerful Christian service. His all-inclusive approach will intrigue and provide the impetus for those willing to pursue the heart of God.

Interfacing Evangelism and Discipleship will change the course of your outreach!

Dr. Timothy M. Hill
General Overseer
Church of God, Cleveland, Tennessee

C.A.P.S. Paradigm

C.A.P.S. Paradigm (Care, Aware, Prepare, Share) is a methodology to evangelism that describes its scope from God's perspective and the individual believer. He wants the believer to examine their heart as it relates to the Great Commission and the words of Jesus. The C.A.P.S. Paradigm introduces only the Great Commission, but I believe the other great instructions from God. I describe this in the figure 1.

Figure 1

Care	The Great Call
Aware	The Great Command
Prepare	The Great Collection
Share	The Great Connection

Additional Notes

The Great Commission

Jesus declares in Matthew 28:18-20,

"And Jesus came and spake unto them, saying, All power is given unto me in heaven and in earth. Go ye therefore, and teach all nations, baptizing them in the name of the Father, and of the Son, and of the Holy Ghost: Teaching them to observe all things whatsoever I have commanded you: and, lo, I am with you always, even unto the end of the world. Amen."

This Commission should be known to every believer.

_____

_____

_____

Jesus is challenging the Church to fulfill its divine call and the reason for its existence.

_____

_____

It is not just a good slogan or spiritual words, it is the mission of the Church.

_____

_____

_____

Additional Notes

Component #1
Care

The Great Call

"For I was an hungred, and ye gave me meat: I was thirsty, and ye gave me drink: I was a stranger, and ye took me in: Naked, and ye clothed me: I was sick, and ye visited me: I was in prison, and ye came unto me."
Matthew 25:35, 36

Evangelism is about reaching the needs of people.

_____
_____
_____

Interfacing Evangelism and Discipleship – Methodology of Evangelism

We operate as true child of God when spread the love of God.

_____
_____
_____

Meeting the needs of people has way of opening doors of people's hearts.

_____
_____
_____

If you want people hear what you have to say about Jesus, show them what you see about their need.

_____
_____
_____

Jesus says, when we do for others, we are doing for Him (Matthew 25:45).

_____
_____
_____

Component #1 Care

There many needs in the world, but Jesus saw fit to identify those who are hungry, thirsty, naked, and need to be visited.

_____

_____

_____

No matter where you are in life, fulling the call to evangelism will come out one of these areas.

_____

_____

_____

Additional Notes

Component #2
Aware

The Great Command

"But ye shall receive power, after that the Holy Ghost is come upon you: and ye shall be witnesses unto me both in Jerusalem, and in all Judaea, and in Samaria, and unto the uttermost part of the earth."

Acts 1:8

Interfacing Evangelism and Discipleship – Methodology of Evangelism

Jesus prophesies to His disciples about the coming power that will assist in fulfillment of God's divine plan for evangelism.

_____
_____
_____

Jesus lets the disciple know that the Holy Spirit will possess them in a supernatural way.

_____
_____
_____

The Holy Spirit will give them power, so they can be witnesses.

_____
_____
_____

Jesus gives a path or outline how the gospel will spread.

_____
_____
_____

Component #2 Aware

Where is your Jerusalem?

_____
_____
_____

Where is your Judea and Samaria?

_____
_____
_____

Where is your uttermost part of the earth?

_____
_____
_____

Acts 1:8 lets us know there are no boundaries to spreading the gospel.

_____
_____
_____

Where is God calling you on the triangle?

_____

_____

_____

Component #2 Aware

Additional Notes

Component #3
Prepare

The Great Collection

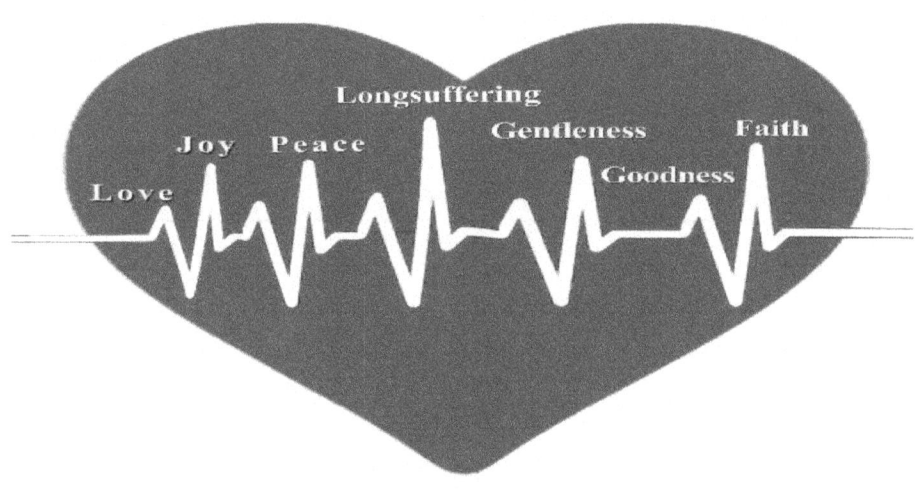

"But the fruit of the Spirit is love, joy, peace, longsuffering, gentleness, goodness, faith, Meekness, temperance: against such there is no law."
Galatians 5:22, 23

Allow God to prepare your heart.
_____
_____
_____

Component #3 Prepare

Pray daily for a heart toward souls.
___
___
___

Operating by the fruit of the Spirit is crucial to evangelism.
___
___
___

The Nature of Fruit:
___
___
___

Love
___
___
___

Joy

_____

_____

_____

Peace

_____

_____

_____

Longsuffering

_____

_____

_____

Gentleness

_____

_____

_____

Component #3 Prepare

Goodness
_____
_____
_____

Faith
_____
_____
_____

Additional Notes

Component #4
Share

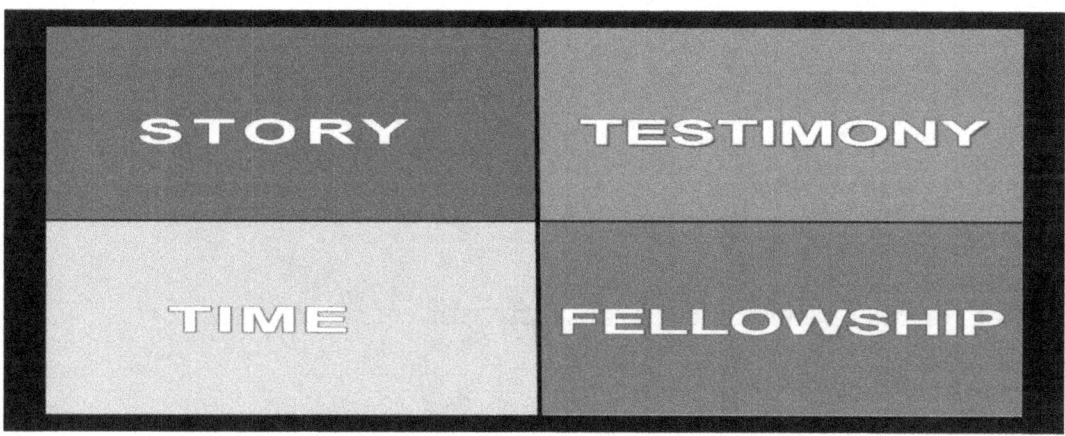

"The woman then left her waterpot, and went her way into the city, and saith to the men, Come, see a man, which told me all things that ever I did: is not this the Christ"
John 4:28, 29

Story

- Everyone has a story about our lives
- Your transparency opens doors of the unbeliever's heart

- What is your story?

___

Testimony

- What is your testimony?
- What darkness did God remove from you?
- How far gone were you?

___

Time

- How much time are you willing to give up for a lost soul?
- What is important to the unbeliever that doesn't compromise your faith?

Fellowship

- One meal may make a world of difference.
- Jesus engaged with the unbeliever, but not conforming to the world.
- Jesus spent most of His time with the publicans and sinners.

Additional Notes

Two By Two Rule

"And he called unto him the twelve, and began to send them forth by two and two, and gave them power over unclean spirit."
Mark 6:7

- To have a witness

_____
_____
_____

- One person is praying.

_____
_____
_____

- Protection

_____
_____
_____

- Connection

_____

_____

_____

Additional Notes

Types of Evangelism

There are various ways we can present the gospel to evangelize and reach souls for the kingdom of God.

How can you, your church, or your ministry utilize the following approaches to build the kingdom of God?

- Church Planting

_____
_____
_____

- Street (Corner, Door-to-Door)

_____
_____
_____

- Outreach (Nursing/Hospital, Prison, Clothing, and Food Pantry)

_____
_____

Types of Evangelism

- Small Groups

- Personal (Job, Home)

- Mall

- Prayer Wash

Additional Notes

About the Author

DR. AARON R. JONES serves as Senior Pastor of New Hope Church of God. Under his pastorate is New Hope Kiddie Kollege, Inc (Daycare) and New Hope Community Outreach Services, Inc. Dr. Jones also oversees New Hope Church of God Ghana (2 churches) and New Hope Church of God Uganda (3 churches).

Dr. Jones is an Ordained Bishop with the Church of God denomination and is the DELMARVA-DC District Overseer (16 churches). Dr. Jones serves on DELMARVA-DC's Regional Council, Ministerial Internship Program Board, Urban Ministry Committee, Finance Committee, and Chaplain's Board. He also serves on both the Church of God's International and DELMARVA-DC Ministry to the Military Board. In his local community, Dr. Jones serves as a Chaplain for the Charles County Sheriff Department. He also serves as Board Secretary for the United Ministers Coalition of Southern Maryland, Inc.

Being obedient to 2 Timothy 2:15, "Study to show thyself approved…," Dr. Jones received a Doctorate in Theology and Pastoral Counseling from Life

Christian University and a Doctorate in Christian Counseling from American Christian College and Seminary. He is a certified Pastoral Counselor with the International Association of Christian Counseling Professionals. He is a Life and Pastoral Coach. He is the former Executive Vice President of the National Bible College and Seminary in Fort Washington, Maryland.

Dr. Jones has published ten books and a soul-wining project that provide a biblical foundation for Christian doctrine and discipline. He has recorded a CD entitled, Peace in the Storm. He is the founder and owner of God's Comfort Ministries, LLC, which provides Christian literature, evangelism training, and spiritual guidance. He has appeared live on TCT Network; WATC-TV's Atlanta Live; Babbie's House (hosted by CCM artist Babbie Mason); and In Concert Today on DCTV. He has done radio interviews with Radio One's WYCB's program; The Praise Fest Show; and online with Total Prayze. He was featured on the cover of Change Gospel Magazine and interviewed on Promoting Purpose Magazine.

Dr. Jones not only serves God, but his country as well. He has served over 20 years in the Armed Forces. He is a retired Chaplain with the Army National Guard. He participated in both Operation Noble Eagle (2003) and Operation Iraqi Freedom III (2005).

Dr. Jones is happily married to the former Sharon Russell. He sincerely believes without her love, support, and encouragement, many of his goals would not have been accomplished.

Contact Page

Mailing Address:
150 Post Office Road #1079
Waldorf, Maryland 20604

Website: www.godscomfort.net

Email: drjones@godscomfortmin.net

Facebook: God's Comfort Ministries

Twitter: @GodsComfort_Min

Instagram: @godscomfort_min

GOD'S COMFORT MINISTRIES

God's Comfort Ministries (GCM) provides practical Christian books, teachings, trainings, and coaching to new converts and seasoned believers. GCM provides understanding of the doctrinal principles of the Bible.

Services Provided

Pastoral and Life Coaching

Evangelism and Discipleship Training

Spiritual Guidance

New Author Consultation

Christian Literature

www.ingramcontent.com/pod-product-compliance
Lightning Source LLC
Chambersburg PA
CBHW081358080526
44588CB00016B/2528